for

....

from

....

here's to mom
a giving and gifted woman
Copyright © 2008 Hallmark Licensing, Inc.

Published by Hallmark Books,
a division of Hallmark Cards, Inc.,
Kansas City, MO 64141
Visit us on the Web at www.Hallmark.com.

Editorial Director: Todd Hafer
Editor: Jeff Morgan
Art Director: Kevin Swanson
Designer: Mary Eakin
Production Artist: Dan Horton

ISBN: 978-1-59530-189-5

BOK4334

Printed and bound in China

here's to
mom
a giving and gifted woman

by Lisa Riggin

GIFT BOOKS
from Hallmark

LISA RIGGIN AND HER MOM

My mom was fond of telling
my seven siblings and me that
she was raising us to be able
to take care of ourselves.

Usually when I heard that, it reminded me to pay attention to whatever we were doing right then – peeling oranges, making beds, memorizing bird calls – because it might be something I was going to need to know. Other times, I think maybe she was just looking forward to getting us all out of the house. Who could blame her?

Now that I'm a mom myself, I realize that preparing children for life on their own is one of the most important jobs a parent has. If you can do that while making sure your child feels loved, there's not much more to it. Simple? Sure. But nobody said it was easy.

So here's to moms everywhere – my own and yours – moms who understood and accepted that raising a child was more than baking cookies and kissing bumped knees and elbows. Because of them, we're out here working, playing, and if we're lucky, loving our own children, knowing that we owe so much to our moms for giving us a solid foundation on which to build our lives.

Lisa Riggin

Lisa Riggin

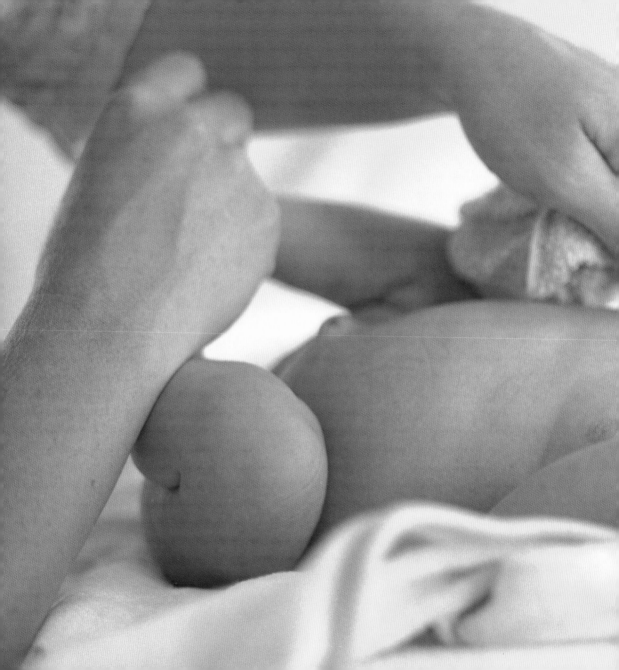

Here's to Mom...
first love,
nurturer,

micro economist,

cheerleader, keeper of secrets,

and protector from

sharp objects.

She's a super mom who healed
small boo-boos
with a kiss and a

okie

and who is still mending bruised egos with only a hug and a giant-sized helping of unconditional love.

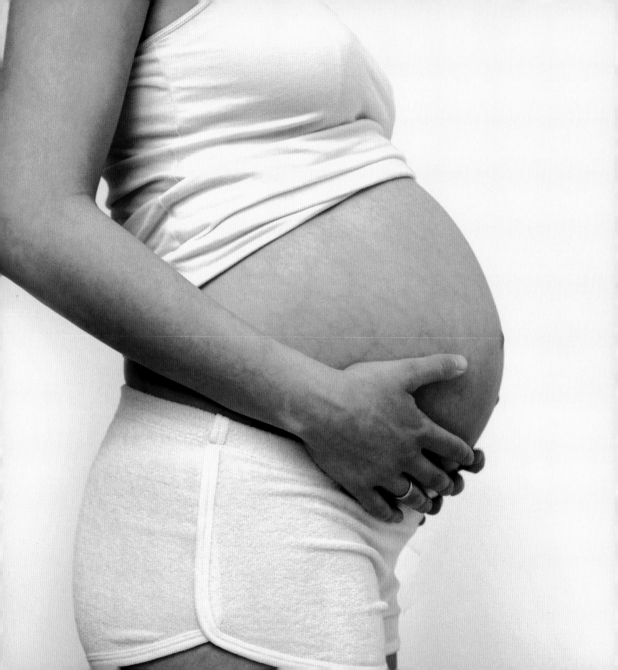

When she first became a mom,
love flowed from her heart
in a way that told her
there would always be
enough to give.

With grace and humor,
       she accepted stretch marks,
burp stains, and

strained
prunes

in her hair –

knowing it was a small price to pay
for the chance to participate in a
miracle.

She's learned that it's okay
to leave the dust bunnies
          and dishes waiting sometimes,
because the really important stuff
          can disappear so fast.

And the food from

Mom's
kitchen,

whether down-home,

gourmet, or out of a box,

still holds that secret ingredient

no one will ever be able to match.

Here's to an understanding mom
who could see that a
little squish of mud between the toes
might be good for the soul. . .

Who understood that raking leaves into the

biggest pile
EVER

and then jumping in and
having to rake them up again
was not a waste of time.

Here's to a giving and gifted woman
who, whenever possible,
made sure her child tasted
the sweet smokiness of a

campfire
s'more...

put lightning bugs in a jar. . .

carved a pumpkin,
built sand castles and snowmen,
searched for four-leaf clovers,
ran through a

sprinkler...

and felt the rush of freewheeling a bike
down a neighborhood hill –
because kids can't really grow up
until they do.

Practical and smart,
Mom can recite 400 uses for

vinegar

and knows the best month
to buy a bedspread.

She's the kind of woman who
cares more about how to

fix it

than how it happened.

And whatever else she may do,
it's clear that Mom –
like all moms –

works

at home.

With an understanding heart,
Mom could hear
    "I didn't ask to be born"
and an hour later dole out
    twenty bucks for the show.

ADMIT ONE

336012

336012

0046

3360

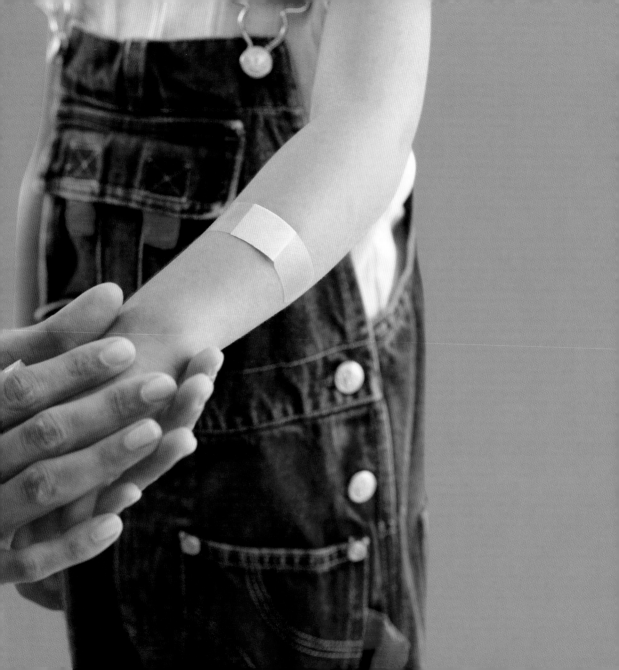

Loving through the terrible twos,
the teen angst, the too-busy times –

she goes on loving through all of life's

ups and downs.

And when you finally understand
something she's told you a hundred times,
she's willing to pretend it was your idea.

No matter how
        capable and confident we get,
                there will always be times

when Mom's reassuring voice
            on the other end of the line
    is the one we most need to hear.

Here's to a woman
    schooled by experience
who has learned to
trust her abilities and offer help
    where it's needed.

She can give

advice...

lend a

hand...

and make sense out of

chaos

while making it look easy —
even when it's not.

And in those times when
it would have been easier to run
from the problems of the world,
she faced them,
knowing that the world
she helped create is where
her children would live.

Both woman of the world and earth mother, Mom is someone who can share her expertise in the boardroom and her

mud pie recipe

with miniature outdoor chefs.

Even if she's the kind of mom
who can build real bridges,
her strongest connections are made
with bridges of love.
In a world of commerce and concrete,
she's out there creating
a better world,
one kindness at a time.

Mom's devotion to family
often means her
"I'm headed
to bed"
includes picking up, checking up,
finishing up, and setting up
before a well-deserved rest.

And if she ever vows to "throw out
      all this crap once and for all,"

it's certain that doesn't include
a single "I love you" finger painting
      or clay pinch pot that
once-little hands made for her.

Mom totally gets it that everybody
needs to do nothing now and then . . .

and she recognizes that there are times
when doing something –
even if it's

not perfect-

is the right thing to do.

Mom also understands the need for
balance and can preach the virtues
of healthy eating while whipping up
a killer three-layer gooey

chocolate
masterpiece

that can make heads spin –
because "food should make you happy."

And when she puts others first,
it's because she knows that
being able to care for others
is one of the greatest pleasures of life.

So here's to Mom –
always there, no matter how far
or in what direction we go.

Because when it comes down
to the important stuff –
whether to start from scratch
or save some time, plunge ahead
or wait for a better moment,

forgive
and forget

or just forgive –

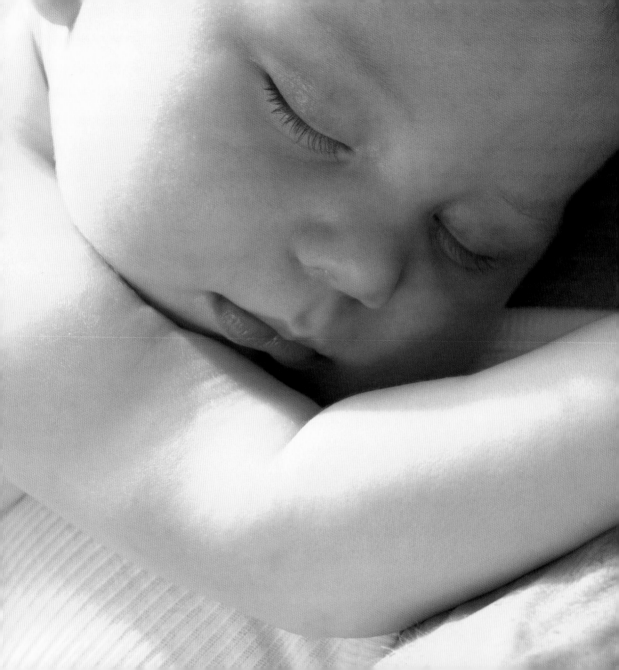

we can listen for the wisdom
of Mom's guiding love
gently whispering
in our hearts.

As a Hallmark writer,
Lisa Riggin is fulfilling a dream
that began in the fifth grade.

She also wanted to become a forest ranger but gave
that up when she saw the uniforms. Leading a simple,
sustainable lifestyle is important to Lisa and her family.
She is studying botanical medicine and is actively involved
in community recycling and environmental awareness
initiatives. She enjoys spending time with her husband
and son, particularly hiking and sailing.

If you have enjoyed this book,
Hallmark would love to hear from you.

Please send your comments to:
Book Feedback, Hallmark Cards, Inc.
Mail Drop 215, 2501 McGee Kansas City, MO 64108

Or e-mail us at booknotes@hallmark.com.